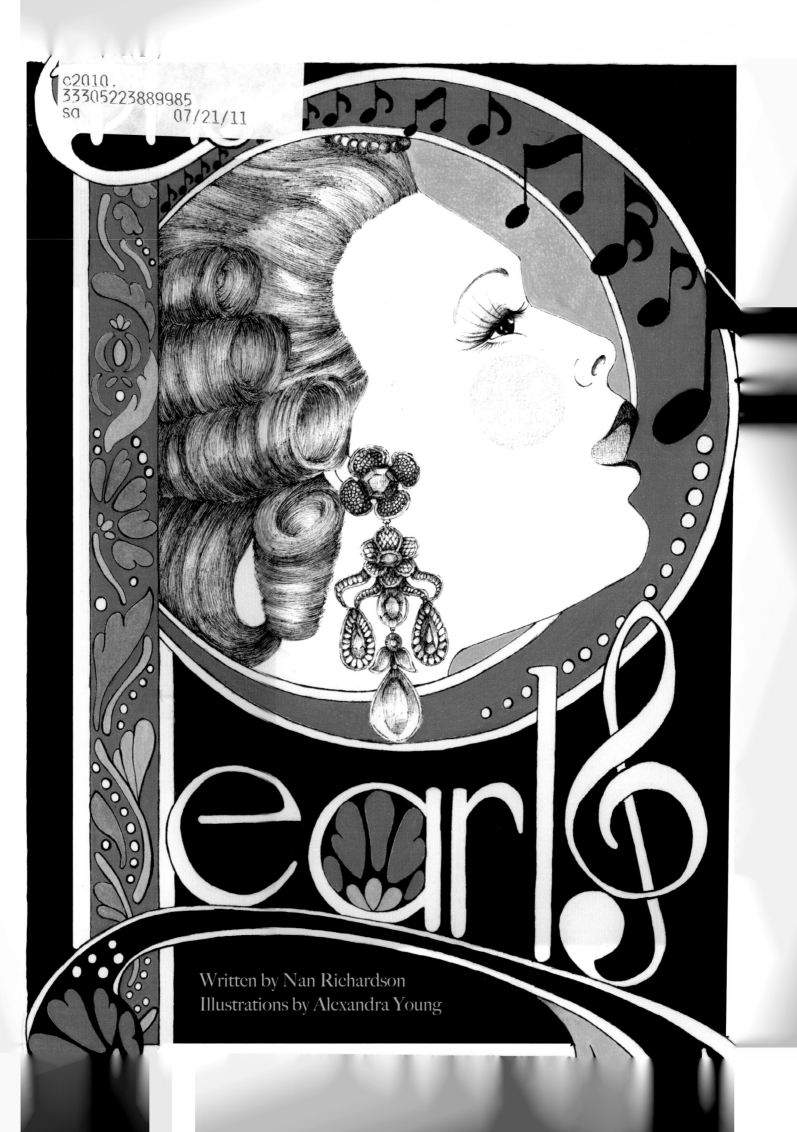

Pearls

Written by Nan Richardson

Illustrations by Alexandra Young

nce upon a time in Russia, Nicolas Cheremeteff was the richest man in the land. He owned castles and lands and 200,000 souls. But more than all his gold and wealth, he loved...music.

He traveled the world—to Paris and London—to see the b

He dreamed of creating his own great stage to rival them a

An old song tells of Nicolas hunting with his dogs in the woods of his estate one day, when he heard a lovely voice singing. He spied a beautiful girl tending her cows and picking gooseberries. "What is your name, pretty one, and who do you belong to?" he asked. "My name is Praskovia," the peasant girl replied, "and I belong to you."

Nicolas was captivated. He took her to one of his palaces and hired tutors to teach her to be a lady. She learned quickly: French and Italian, literature and history, dancing and deportment. And most of all, he nurtured her lovely voice.

Praskovia was ready for her debut.
Nicolas and his father Peter had built a
magnificent opera theater in the Kuskovo
palace. There Praskovia sang: a triumph!
Nicolas decided to give his actors special
names—Irina was "The Sapphire", Tatiana
"The Garnet"—and crowned Praskovia
"The Pearl" for her shining, luminous
talent and pure heart.

In honor of Catherine the Great, the Cheremeteffs hosted
a grand fête in Kuskovo. The table was covered with gold,
silver, and precious stones. Cannons roared, torches blazed,
maidens in white strew flowers on the paths, and gondolas
sailed the lake. Praskovia sang her heart out, telling the story
of a girl who fights the world for what is rightfully hers. The
empress, enthralled, gave The Pearl a huge diamond ring.

Nicolas and Praskovia grew even closer and
his love for her grew stronger. They moved into a charming cottage
on the estate, where they lived simply and quietly, and she worked at
what she loved: embroidery and many acts of kindness to the poor.

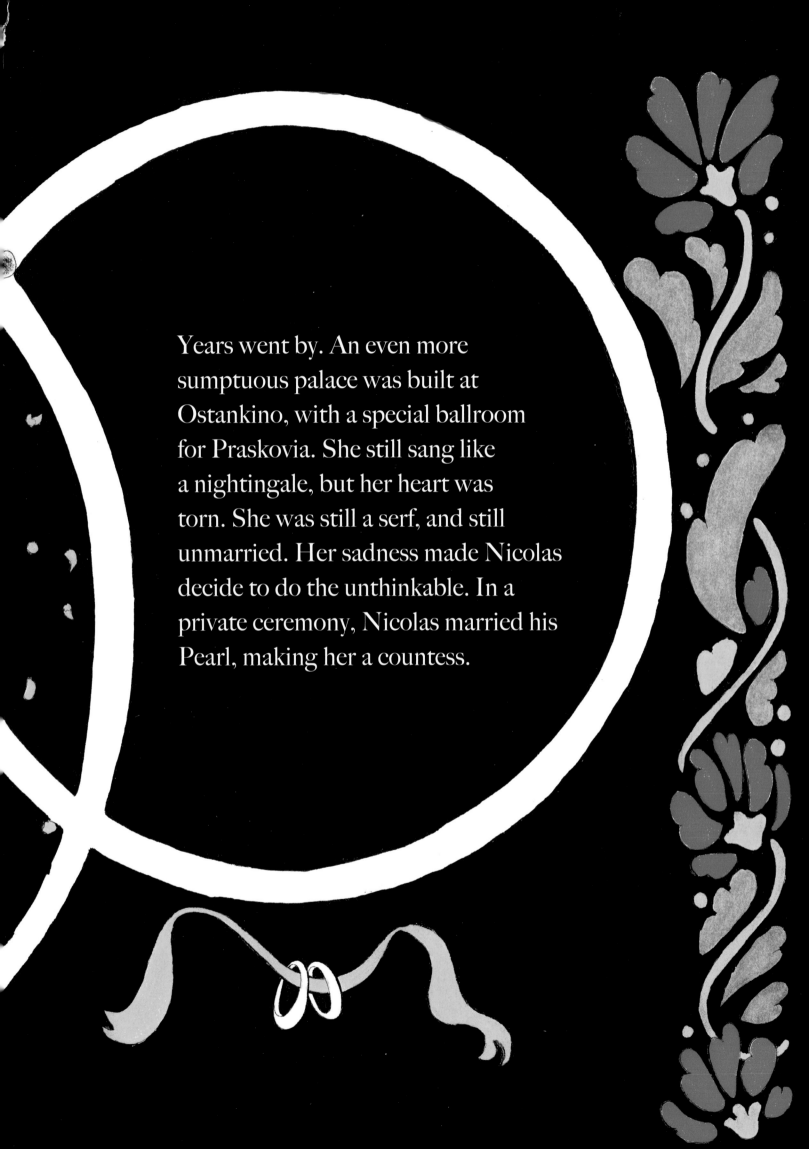

Years went by. An even more sumptuous palace was built at Ostankino, with a special ballroom for Praskovia. She still sang like a nightingale, but her heart was torn. She was still a serf, and still unmarried. Her sadness made Nicolas decide to do the unthinkable. In a private ceremony, Nicolas married his Pearl, making her a countess.

Happiness, though sweet, was short-lived. Praskovia soon gave birth to a healthy baby boy named Dmitri, but a month later she suddenly took ill and died. A distraught Nicolas cried, "I have lost my guiding star," and took a lock of her hair to wear around his neck.

Her funeral was magnificent. Black horses with gold embroidered cloths marched along the Nevsky Prospect in St. Petersburg to the monastery where she would be buried. Two hundred singers, priests, officers, and serfs turned out for the procession, for Praskovia's kindness made her beloved by the people. Crowds gathered to watch the grandest funeral St. Petersburg had seen in years. The scandalized nobles just peered from behind their silk curtains.

In Praskovia's memory, Nicolas completed
the hospital they had worked on together,
the Almhouse, in Sukharevskaya Square. It
was a place where the poor and sick could
go and receive good care. In its gallery was
a statue of The Pearl, where each year, on
Praskovia's name day, orphan girls received
a dowry so they could marry...

So the beautiful Pearl was remembered
forever, for her goodness, for her great gift
of song, and for bringing joy and comfort
to others.

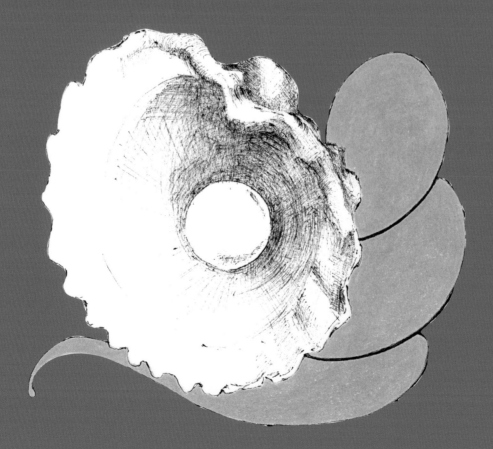

To Isabel and James, my little gems!
And their cousins, Alexandra and
Andrew Cheremeteff Richardson,
descendants of The Pearl.
• Nan Richardson •

For a friend that is so A, B, and C.
• Alexandra Young •

NOTES

Pg. 3. The popular song appears to have no factual basis, but conforms to the many archetypes of accidental meetings between kings and fair maidens (as in *Sleeping Beauty* or *Snow White*).

Pg. 5. Her first role was as Gubert in the comic opera *L'Amitié à l'épreuve* by André Grétry.

Pg. 6. Her first starring role was in Antonio Sacchini's opera *La colonie*. She went on to star in many operas, including Monsigny's *Le Déserteur* and *Aline, reine de Golconde*, Paisiello's *L'infante de Zamora*, Rousseau's *Le devin du village*, and Piccinni's *La buona figliuola maritata*. Her most important role was Eliane in Grétry's opera, *Les mariages samnites*, where she sang for the first time in 1785 (for Catherine the Great) and went on to star for twelve years—including a bravura performance before Stanisław August Poniatowski, the last king of Poland. In 1795, to open the great theater at Ostankino, she premiered the opera *Zelmira and Smelon*, or *The Capture of Izmail*, where she acted in the role of the captive Turkish woman Zelmira.

Pg.10. The words on the plaque on Praskovia's grave begin:

> This plain marble, unfeeling and impermanent / Hides the priceless remains of a wife and mother.
> Her soul was a temple of virtue / In which peace, piety, and faith resided / Where pure love and friendship dwelt…

For an authoritative history, we refer you to Douglas Smith's biography, *The Pearl* (Yale University Press, 2008), that is rich in both meticulous research and fascinating detail.

ACKNOWLEDGMENTS

With grateful thanks to the Cheremeteff Family, notably Kyra Cheremeteff and her father Count Nikita Cheremeteff, whose kindness is unsurpassed, and who offered their informed advice unstintingly and graciously. And in warm acknowledgment of the generosity and support of Sidney Kimmel.

The Pearl

An Umbrage Editions Book

First Edition
10 9 8 7 6 5 4 3 2 1
ISBN 978-1-884167-24-9

Umbrage Editions, Inc.
111 Front Street, Suite 208
Brooklyn, New York 11201
www.umbragebooks.com

An Umbrage Editions book
Publisher: Nan Richardson
Associate Editor: Antonia Blair
Office Manager: Valerie Burgio
Editorial Assistant: Daniel Wilson
Copy Editor: Amanda Bullock
Editorial Intern: Samantha Richardson
Design and Production: Tanja Geis
Scans: DOT Editions, Brooklyn

Distributed by Consortium in the United States. www.cbsd.com

Distributed by Turnaround in Europe. www.turnaround-co.uk

Printed in Iceland by Oddi